# The Lyth of Lemmings

By Frank Mueller

Copyright © 2007, Frank J. Mueller

ISBN: 978-0-6151-9913-9

Published by Lulu Press

**Table of Contents**

Chapter 1   *What is a Lyth?*

Chapter 2   *If there are no Solutions, then there are no Problems...*

Chapter 3   *Donkeys, Mules, Decision Makers and Slime Mold*

Chapter 4   *The Need for Critical Thinking Skills*

Chapter 5   *Religion: "The Foundation of most of our Mythos"*

Chapter 6   *Technological Growth and Religion*

Chapter 7   *Why does one become a member of a Violent Fundamentalist Cult?*

Chapter 8   *Logos versus Mythos*

Chapter 9   *Why do you think Discrimination exists in religious settings?*

Chapter 10   *Did Buddha have Faith?*

Chapter 11   *Religious Pluralism and Interfaith Dialogue "Some Thoughts"*

Chapter 12 *Science: "Is Science always Logical?" "How our Mythos has influenced Science?"*

Chapter 13 *Social Aspects of Lyths: "What effect has Mythos had on our behavior?"*

Chapter 14 *Are all Cultures driven by a Mythos?*

## Criteria for a Lyth

It appears we have more lyths than most people are aware of and so I am asking for help. I have defined criteria to ascertain lyths. It is basically this: when we believe in things that we can neither prove nor disprove and we base our actions, beliefs and morals on them and those actions, beliefs and morals make it so that others are subjugated than the mythos has produced a lyth.

*At some point in time, I am looking to produce an "elementary table" similar to the table we use to describe the known physical elements in our environment.*

First thing is to define a "lyth" is to define myth or some form of mythic thinking.

## Myth or Mythic Thinking Defined

What makes a myth a myth? It is because the premise it is based on cannot be proved nor disproved. I have used the example of slavery and belief concerning souls. Slavers used the belief system that promoted the idea slaves had no souls. This allowed them to appease their conscience and the conscience of the society they supported. It gave them a false sense of superiority and if the slaves believed the premise a false sense of inferiority. In your submission of Lyths that you have found, first you will need to be able to define the premise of the mythic thinking as to how it cannot be "proved" or "disproved." As in the example given; there has never been a proof shown that any type of soul exists or has ever existed. It is a belief that has no supporting fact to prove it. I am not saying it is a "bad belief" nor am I saying that the belief in souls is thus wrong or is inherently flawed in any way. What I am saying is that it has no validity in fact or demonstrative evidence to prove it as fact. Second, is defining what a "Lyth" is and how it affects our society.

How is this mythos or mythic thinking used to harm our society, creating an unfair circumstance or process for individuals?

When we use arbitrary beliefs that may or may not be true to base our actions for, against, or with other people we will usually come up with actions that seem unfair to most people. The idea that "slaves had no souls" was used to say that the people who were enslaved could be brutalized because they were to be considered as things. Because the mythic thinking that was used is that things do not have souls. We can eat things, hunt things and use things to do whatever we want with because they are things and not humans. In the case of the slaves, it allowed the slave owners to rape, murder, herd, breed, and use those people in any brutal way they could think of and under any conditions imaginable. A "Lyth" is a lie that has come from mythic thinking. The lie has no basis in fact. The lie is used to hide the truth. The lie is used in an effort to maintain power or to subjugate people in such a way as to get power without due process.

The intent of my research and writing is to use Collective Wisdom to uncover mythic thinking that may be holding societies back or may be in some cases actually allowing them to prosper. Not "all" mythic thinking is bad; it may seem illogical when in fact it is "a-logical." One can look at Logic as one looks at Morals if we take "innovation" into consideration. In studying morality there is moral, immoral and amoral. Moral is that which the society has deemed to be good and beneficial to the growth of the society. Immoral, on the other hand is that which destroys or in some way, makes a society deteriorate as a whole. Amoral, is the phenomenon that occurs when what is observed does not fit in either of the first two categories. We often refer to small children as "being" amoral because they have not yet learned society's morals. They have no "intent" of doing wrong. Thus, their actions are amoral instead of being immoral.

Myths are stories that normally cannot be proved or disproved. They usually deal with aspects of reality that seem truly incredible such as monsters, fairies, elves, gods and phenomenon that are next to impossible in our reality.

We can each have our own unique perspective on the truth. The thing is having a unique perspective is like having an accent; each of us can say the very same thing in a very different way. This is relative truth; now absolute truth exists as represented by the fact that although we each are saying the same thing in a different way: we are each saying the same thing. None of us owns the absolute truth. When we share with each other, our objective perspectives it allows us to get a better glimpse of it though our collective views.

You will hear this again: "Imagine all of us looking at the sky...we are all looking at a specific star...since one of you is in Florida, one in Virginia and so on, we all see the same star from a different perspective. It will have a different hue or color because of the different atmospheric conditions we each see it through...however, we all see a star...if one person says they see a cow...will that will cause it to become a cow?" No, it will not make it become a cow. The truth when known brings about a certainty of knowledge that does not lead to self-righteousness and angry mannerisms.

Having a small group of people who are knowledgeable on a subject combined with a large group who are interested and have the basic facts can as a group when directed properly come up with a solution to problems that to most seem irresolvable and often are to mere individuals. We eventually will be using a variety of surveys, focus groups, co-relational studies, empirical comparative analysis grids.

How You Become a Co-Author or Author of your own work concerning the subject

Here is the web site for submission of your work.

http://thelythoflemmings.neuralpreneural.com

If it is accepted, you will be directed to a web site that will allow you to set up your work on it. Your work will be featured in this book. If you want, you can then write more on the topic of your choice. This work will be sold through this book as well as from your web site.

What You Need TO DO NOW

Guidelines for Submitting Proposed Material for this Book

The Work You are Submitting

Brief description: In one or two paragraphs, describe the work, its approach and your purpose in writing. Outstanding features: List briefly, what you consider outstanding or unique features of the work. Will the work include summaries, examples, cases, questions, problems, etc.? Supplements: Do you plan to provide supplementary material such as a manual, study guide, video's, software or the like? Level: For whom is the work intended and what is the level? What are the student prerequisites, if any? Has the material been class-tested? If not, will it be?

Your Background

Please provide a description of your background, relevant professional activities, and number of times you have taught a course if any, and other writing experience. Please attach a copy of your vita, resume or 5 (five) paragraph biography. Do you have other writing plans when this project is complete?

The Competition

Top three books in the field concerning the topic of your materiel: How does your work compare and/or contrast with them? Please discuss each competing work in a separate paragraph. Include author, title, publisher, publication date, length, and price (if known). Please focus on comparing topical coverage, organization, level, writing style, art program, pedagogy, and any other relevant similarities and differences between your project and the competing books. Be frank: This information is written for reviewers, providing them with a comparative framework and should accurately reflect your views. Are you aware of any similar works in progress but unpublished?

The Market

What is the primary audience for which your work is intended? What other "audiences" such as a "college level class" would it serve? Would the work be appropriate for international, high school, or trade markets? What is your expectation of the size of the market? If you have done any market research of your own, I would appreciate receiving a brief summary of your findings.

The Outline

The outline provides an overview of the entire work. It is a road map guiding both the reviewer and the publisher along your specific point of view. Chapter heads (if you have chapters) should be followed by subheads that explain the content at a greater level of detail. Paragraphs should be used as needed to clarify the outline. If revision of the sample material is requested, always provide a revised outline.

The Sample Chapters or Writings

The sample chapters or writings should illustrate the strongest and most distinctive aspects of your work. Selected chapters or writings should include what best represents your work's basic idea, its quality, and distinctive features. Prepare the material carefully. If the work is full of typographical or grammatical errors, the attention will be diverted from the more important consideration of content. If your work features problems or exercises, please include some samples.

Additional Information

Final pieces of information to round out the proposal: What schedule of completion do you have in mind for your book? Please remember that the initial deadline for the First Edition is in May of 2007. What will be the approximate length of your work? Please state whether your estimate is in book or manuscript pages. If dealing in manuscript pages, please describe length in terms of 81/2" X 11" double spaced pages. What kind of art is needed for your work? What is the estimated number of line drawings and photographs? (Please look at competing works for a frame of reference.) Is the manuscript being prepared on word processing software? I am using Microsoft Word. Please list the names and affiliations of qualified reviewers who could be asked to critique the work if you know of any.

Do you have any other questions or comments? Please contact me with them as they come to you. If you would like to submit this in another manner let me know. Your work if accepted will be entered as a part of a collection on this topic and marketed as such.

Where to send submissions:

http://thelythoflemmings.neuralpreneural.com/

## *What is a Lyth?*

Lyth is a word that I made up. It stands for something that is a lie that became a myth. Myths influence the way in which large groups of humans think and even sometimes process information. Myths are the underlying patterns that influence our "Mythos," and our mythos is our own take on spirituality. A myth may or may not be accurate or true. It is normally seemingly impossible to prove or disprove a myth. Most myths began as allegories to describe what appears to the listener as the ineffable. Many myths begin by someone who believes they understand something or some phenomenon using faulty reasoning. Some myths began in order to gain or keep control over a certain type of people. When it is clear, a myth began as a way of gaining control over people I call that a "Lyth." A lyth is a myth and a lie combined in order to subjugate. For instance, when the slavers said of the slaves that they kidnapped that "they had no souls."

Below are some web sites that deal with discerning by reason between fact and fallacy.

Fallacy Files

http://www.fallacyfiles.org/

Tecktonics

http://www.tektonics.org/guest/fallacies.html#700

Nizkor

http://www.nizkor.org/features/fallacies/index.html

In 1958 there was a documentary done for Disney called "White Wilderness." In it they showed scenes of Lemmings, small rodents, jumping off of cliffs. The whole thing was made up. Lemmings do not commit suicide. However, it had been shown in countless High Schools as if it were fact. A generation grew up believing that Lemmings commit suicide. They often use the metaphor judgmentally that a group of people is acting like Lemmings.

See this site for more details:
http://www.snopes.com/disney/films/lemmings.htm

*Discussion Question*

What is the importance of "myth" to our society historically and currently?

## *If there are no Solutions, then there are no Problems...*

This was something I learned early in life. When we sense there is a problem or when we have factual evidence of a problem and can describe it and yet we believe there is no solution we are overlooking the obvious. For problems that seem to be irresolvable, what we have is a lack of knowledge "not an irresolvable problem."

We cannot become aware of the existence of a "possible" problem without the backdrop of some sort of a solution. It is similar to how our eyes see light and shadows. If there were no light, we would not see any shadows. There might not be enough light to make out what is in the shadows yet that does not make the shadowy figure disappear. What is needed to have any inkling, intuition, hypothesis, or guess that a problem exists is some form of a possible solution to make the shadow of the problem visible to our mind.

The clinical psychologists N.H. Azrin, R.R. Hutchinson, and D.F. Drake demonstrated through multiple studies using rats in a maze that frustration generates rage. (Bloom, 1995) When the rat was trained to go through the maze and get their cheese and had successfully done so on their own. If a piece of Plexiglas was placed between them and the cheese, they became frustrated. If there were anything near them when they got frustrated, they would brutalize it, regardless of whether it was an inanimate object or if it was one of their family members.

This phenomenon has been shown to exist in humans, apes, chimpanzees, squirrels, fish and the list goes on extensively. What happens with humans is that we form a symbiosis with other humans. We use the maze of social etiquette, of shared belief systems to acquire our proverbial cheese, whatever that may be now.

Humans have a tendency of labeling things they learn about, especially if it gives them a sense of awe. They will then classify them in groups; upon doing that they prioritize the phenomenon. They then organize it, and this is seen and done on our social settings. Richard Dawkins (1982) came up with the name "memes," Jung called it the "collective unconscious," (1976) Eric Berne called it the "script" (1976). It is also called our cosmogony, worldview, or colloquially "the way people see the world."

Matthew Alper (1998) in his book "The God Part of the Brain" postulated that we have within our brain a biological urge to seek a supernatural explanation: That we "may be innately wired to perceive such universal concepts as a spiritual realm, a God, a Soul, and an Afterlife." This could support both the claims of the Atheist as well as the claims of the Theist, Non-Theistic (e.g. Buddhism) and the Deist. If it is fact though, it does help in our understanding of the proverbial "maze."

There is a difference between faith and belief. Faith is what we feel and hold to psychologically when we have no evidence other than our own experiential feelings and thoughts to prove something. "Belief" on the other hand is when we do have evidence that we can demonstrate to others. We can look at our history books and we trust the authors to be telling the truth. We find statements from others about what occurred in the past. We can believe them or we can disbelieve them. Faith in this instance is not required. For example, whether Jesus Christ existed and actually was crucified and the major point for most Christians is whether there was a resurrection from the dead. This is a point of belief, not faith. It is a point of belief based on the testimony of those who were there at the time. Faith enters in when someone believes in something there is no demonstrable material evidence to support the belief.

People, like the rat in the maze get frustrated. When we act as a group, we normally will take out our frustration on another "group." Outsiders are normally labeled for instance, the Jews labeled them Gentiles, the Muslims labeled them Infidels, the Christians called them Heathens, and Atheists label them Idiots. We then classify them by their atrocities, and prioritize their overall value in order to organize our efforts as a group to "change the enemy." In this group process of the Karpman Triangle (victim, abuser, rescuer) (Orriss, 2004) the meaning of important words change: For instance Justice: Justice to someone who is in "victim state of mind" is used to show others what the abusers are taking away from them. As soon as the victim group is in charge, they then become the abuser and punish their enemy for their wrongful deeds. Which brings us to "Peace," this word changes its meaning for those who are in the "rescuer state of mind." Peace is what is found if everyone will only believe as "they" believe. Once this occurs they can resume their rightful status at the head of the "pecking order" and all will be well for everyone. Freedom is the last word representing the malleable concepts involved here. Freedom is that which is normally used as a rallying cry for those in the "abuser state of mind" as they begin using actual physical acts of aggression against "the enemy."

What do you think the rat would do if it had the ability of innovation and could look for new ways to get the cheese? If it had reflectivity and knew or sensed it was in "a maze" controlled by humans? If we can see the possibility of solutions then we can raise our standards instead of merely "trying to be better than" someone else's standards. If we can see our belief system, we can alter it. If we cannot, it alters us.

## Donkeys, Mules, Decision Makers and Slime Mold

There are two basic type of cells Prokaryotes and Eukaryotes. The Eukaryotic cells are far more complex. In the simplest and earliest form of cell biology reproduction is done by passing genetic structure through *replication*. It is similar to someone learning by memorizing and repeating. The Eukaryotic cells were the first to develop a "division of labor" in responsibility. This act changed replication into procreation. The cell did this by incorporating other parts of prokaryotic cells. The first developments of "male and female" are postulated to have occurred in the Eukaryotic cell approximately 720 million years ago (Silva & Moe, 2000-2004). This event occurred in plasmodia slime mold. What if, just imagine for a moment: What if there was someone that somehow "intuited" this lets say 10,000 years ago. They wanted to explain it to others. How do they do it? Do they start talking about a science of biology that does not even exist yet? No, that would be senseless, they write in a manner that could be understood. They tell it in a story.

There are many levels of intuition. Most intuition is developed over time through the study and activities that make complex and abstract concepts commonplace knowledge to those who use them. They then usually overlook how they came to conclusions that are often correct, precise and effective while others are still consulting their textbooks. Then there is the type of intuition that allows the person to extrapolate from known knowledge. In a way, this intuition is developing a "periodic table" as did Dmitri Mendeleev. Dmitri first has to clarify that there were individual "elements" this was a critical event. The enigma that ensued was an observation of natural classification giving elements symmetry in what appeared to be chaos. A French geologist named A.E. Beguyer de Chancourtis in 1862 did the first attempt at a table. This was aided by the discovery of what was called the "*Law of Triads*" postulated by Johann Dobereiner in 1817 and then proven in 1829 through discoveries of the event in such compounds as chlorine, bromine, and iodine and lithium, sodium and potassium. The elements properties showed that the middle elements properties had an average of the other two members when ordered by their atomic weights.

Then John Newland noticed what became known as the "*Law of Octaves*" where there was a physical analogy to the seven intervals of the "*musical scale*." The law stated that any given element would exhibit analogous behavior to the eighth element following it on the periodic table. (1997)

The complexity of intuitive phenomenon grows as interactions increase and utility of information improves. One can extrapolate the creation of certain ideas when one has developed what may be seen as an "ideation periodic table." There is a dramatic increase in complexity in systemic structures as ones observation goes from elements, to cellular structures to multi-cellular structures such as you and me. Ideas like languages have their "elements." Some are referring to these elements as Dawkins mimetic structures others as semiotics (2003). Most ideation is based on what we know or what we believe. More of our actions are determined by what we believe than by what we know. We use valid assumptions and non-valid assumptions. People who lack education often refer to all assumptions as if they are non-valid. This disregards the knowledge they have as well as the knowledge of others. It then makes their assumptions far easier to confuse with actual knowledge. The donkey is an animal that has entered into religion, myth, literature, film, fable and folklore, proverbs and idiomatic expressions, even used as insults when likened to human behavior. The donkey is a mix between a mule and a horse. (Olsen, 1998) It is somewhat the "average" between the two. Horses have 64 chromosomes and mules have 63 chromosomes producing a donkey with 62 chromosomes. The donkey is normally infertile. In western culture, the "idea of the donkey" is used as an insult to those who make assumptions. This is normally done by using another name for the donkey, that of "ass." One would say in a play on words, "to make an assumption makes an ass out of you and me." This overlooks and diminishes the effectiveness of making a valid assumption. A valid assumption is represented by theories and to some degree, fables. Fables carry with them injunctions on behavior that promote certain beliefs found to give a higher probability of protecting or maintaining life as it is known to those who use the fables. Assumption is inherent in imagination, and the ability to imagine is a part of strategic thinking. Strategic thinkers have had a clear advantage over those who fail to "cognitively plan" their futures.

## *The Need for Critical Thinking Skills*

*Critical Reasoning*

The ability to separate our logos or critical reasoning from our mythos or those things we do not understand, cannot prove, and believe without question is what I believe allows "the crowd" to remain independent, and decentralized. Reasoning skills and the ability to reason is a global or universal phenomenon. The problem arises when one attributes faulty logical deductions as reasoning. This is a common denominator in terrorist belief systems. The term "collective wisdom" that I used is used in the sense that James Surowiecki (2004) used when he wrote the book, "The Wisdom of Crowds." This talks of the ability that groups of humans have in figuring things out when given the proper opportunity. Many people have tried to define collective intelligence. Most have called it a name of their own choice. Howard Bloom (2000) called it the "global mind."

Carl Gustav Jung labeled it the "collective unconscious." These shared attributes make up our species as a whole. The problems that arise when we *apply* or *observe order* in the human condition is that we often superimpose our belief system onto what we observe. This is normal when one person is making observations or when a tight group suffering from "groupthink" as Irving Janis (1982) called it imposes a hidden political agenda. We have a tendency as humans to judge the infinite through the use of finite tools, e.g. the unexplainable with the already accepted explanations.

Web Site Resources

Overview of Critical Thinking

http://www.coping.org/write/percept/critical.htm

How to Improve Your Thinking Skills

http://www.psychology4all.com/Thinking.htm

Misconceptions in Critical Thinking that harm our Education System

http://www.criticalthinking.org/resources/articles/diversity.shtml

Critical Thinking and Collaborative Learning

http://sll.stanford.edu/projects/tomprof/newtomprof/postings/173.html

Common Misconception about Critical Thinking

http://everything2.com/index.pl?node_id=433794

Myths and Misunderstanding about Critical Thinking

http://profmulder.home.att.net/intromyths.htm

FREE BOOKS ON CRITICAL THINKING

http://www.questia.com/library/education/curriculum-and-instruction/teachingcritical-thinking.jsp

CRITICAL THINKING RUBRIC

http://www.neiu.edu/~ctl/bulletins/Bulletin11.pdf

CRITICAL THINKING STRATEGIES

http://www.ntlf.com/html/lib/suppmat/103chap7.pdf

CRITICAL THINKING ASSESSMENT

http://classweb.howardcc.edu/jbell/booklets/Ch1_Critical_Thinking_F01.pdf

http://cade.athabascau.ca/vol13.2/bullen.html

http://www.provost.cmich.edu/assessment/posters/assessing%20critical%20thinking.pdf

ARMY

http://www.amsc.belvoir.army.mil/roy.html

COURSE OUTLINE

http://www.etsu.edu/criticalthinking/default.asp

EXERCISES

http://www.unc.edu/depts/wcweb/pdf/critical_thinking_exercises.pdf

MONSTERS

http://www.class.uidaho.edu/crit_think/8-App.htm

CRITICAL THINKING AND MYTH

http://www.abarnett.demon.co.uk/atheism/tooth.html

http://atheism.about.com/od/bookreviews/fr/HoaxesMyths.htm

http://atheism.about.com/od/aboutskepticism/Skepticism_Skeptical_Investigations_and_Critical_Thinking.htm

http://www.gravee.com/search/critical_thinking_on_cultural_myth

http://www.hull.ac.uk/studyadvice/resources/acadw/01pdfs/crithink.pdf

http://colmsmyth.blogspot.com/2006/08/guide-to-critical-thinking.html

http://www.skepdic.com/essays/haskins.pdf

http://www.niu.edu/assessment/Toolkit/vol4_ish1.pdf

http://www.criticalthinking.org/resources/articles/diversity.shtml

http://www.mythinglinks.org/reference~teachers.html

http://www.enemies.com/gnostic-links/critical-thinking.html

http://www.safarix.com/0132203030/ch01lev1sec6

## Religion: "The Foundation of most of our Mythos"

Millions believe in God. A real belief in God would necessitate "faith" since the existence of God is not provable. There are many things that we take for granted that cannot be proved. Take the idea of "cold," an example I have used before. We measure temperature by measuring energy. Thus, we can only measure heat. What we are doing is measuring the levels of heat or "energy." When we say something is cold, we are saying the level of heat energy is at a certain point. We have not yet been able to devise technology that will measure the "absence" of energy.

The idea of individuation as a source of health is a commonly held belief. Having people order us around is not fun. Believing we are "suckers", in some way being devalued, or taking a lower position on "the Pecking Order" seems to present most creatures with fear. Most myths emanate from our view of power. Karen Armstrong (2005) in her book "A Short History of Mythology" said that most myths have five aspects: First, they are rooted in our perception of death and a fear of extinction.

Second, myths become incomprehensible outside of some form of "liturgical drama" reenacted through a ritual. Third, they normally focus on extremes that take us beyond our normal experience. Fourth, myth carries injunctions that guide "social behavior." Fifth, it makes the invisible tangible.

As individuals we want to stay alive, we want to reproduce offspring. We have to consume other living organisms to stay alive. The organisms we eat are normally alive at the molecular level at minimum. We thus "kill" plants and animals and then process them for consumption. We maintain this "pecking order" in order to maintain life. We develop social systems that seem to mimic this pecking order. Staying alive is also seen then, as staying on top of the pecking order.

Myths or rather "Lyths" then, often are used to perpetuate the power of one group over another. The problem it creates is that it dulls the senses and the sensibility of those involved, particularly those who are at the bottom of the pecking order. It creates a "scarcity mentality" in all of the participants that limits our ability to actually deal with the reality of scarcity and known limitations as a group.

As civilizations, grow their ability to comprehend abstractions increases quantitatively in proportion to their collective wisdom or shared knowledge. Advanced civilizations encompass a larger range of variety and in larger groups, their individuals become multivariate rather than multiplicitous or even duplicitous. In 1980, Alvin Toffler (author of "Future Shock") produced a book called "The Third Wave" assessing the positive points that were a part of the current period of crisis. In it he brought out the importance of " (Toffler, 1985) social memory" and how it is being revolutionized by the changes in the "info-sphere", (pp 192-193). He points out:

**"Our remarkable ability to file and retrieve shared memories is the secret of our species' evolutionary success. And anything that significantly alters the way we construct, store, or use social memory therefore touches on the wellsprings of destiny. Twice before, in history humankind has revolutionized its social memory. Today, in constructing a new info-sphere, we are poised on the brink of another such transformation... What makes the leap to a Third Wave info-sphere so historically exciting *is* that it not only vastly expands social memory again, but resurrects it from the dead. The computer, because it processes the data it stores, creates an historically unprecedented situation: it makes social memory both extensive and active. And this combination will prove to be propulsive"**. (6, pp 192-193)

(Judge, 1980) Unlike earlier hopes for a "world brain", a functioning information infrastructure is emerging very rapidly which will accomplish much more than was desired by those who first reflected on the future of information. (Recent years have nevertheless seen the rebirth of a World Mind Group. But Toffler makes the point that:

**"Unless we incinerate the planet and our social memory with it, we shall before long have the closest thing to a civilization with total recall"** (6, p 193).

Compassionate societies offer more "alternatives" to their members to deal with scarcity even allowing for technological growth, which is an outward expression of their inner logic. This is different from the autocratic societies who live with an either-or mentality of looking at the world as merely a cruel and harsh place that demands of them lying, cheating, stealing and even murder. The best lie or the best lyth is 99% truth. That 1% keeps it from accurately performing. If there are no solutions, then there are no problems. We have to have the shadow of a solution to become aware of a problem. We might "intuit" it, such as the existence of "God, god, or a supernatural force"; or deduce it, such as the existence of cold.

Most sentient beings when they do not readily see an answer to their dilemma get frustrated. The frustration we feel can lead us to despair and then reflectivity or can lead to depression and then anger. To say, "there is no absolute truth" is a statement that is posited as an absolute truth that says in and of itself that "it" does not exist. It is somewhat like, and please do not confuse the analogy with the people involved, like a child who holds their hands over their face and says, "You can't see me!" in a high-pitched voice. We sometimes have a tendency of saying something we do not understand does not exist. The dilemma here is that; just because we do not understand or are even unable to measure something: Is that proof that it does not exist?

## *Technological Growth and Religion*

As countries modernize, they experience change with varying degrees of conflict involved. Countries that have modernization occur rapidly are hotbeds for Fundamentalist movements. They are especially vulnerable if they are Third World Nations, who lack a system of national education. There appears to be a strong correlation to technological/educational growth to religious abatement (MacCulloch, Pezzini).

As Europe and America moved into the Industrial age, they did their changes gradually. Each technological improvement brought about a correspondent change in their overall social make-up. The reliance on mythos faded or sublimated to the use of reason. Luther saw the emergence of reason as a detriment to the growth of Christianity that it would lead to Atheism. Calvin saw it as an empirically supporting the Christian doctrinal beliefs and so did John Wesley who brought about the "Methodical Christian Approach" and the Methodist church (Armstrong).

Karen Armstrong proposed that the very reasoning they use to understand the significance of religion and faith has blinded secularists and those who follow the scientific rationalistic approach to life (Scientific Materialism). The secularist approach has led to an arrogance that kept them in a position of trying to "be right" when "doing right" was needed for understanding. That these theologies and ideologies may be rooted in fear is apparent, but modern secularism is the culprit, having drained life of its meaning and purpose. With the encroachment of secular ideologies, a form of paranoia erupts in highly religious peoples. When the interpretations of meaning behind discoveries are prone to dismantle long held unquestioned suppositions about reality, fear is inevitable. As millions of people around the globe struggle with seemingly irreconcilable philosophies of life, the rise of militant fundamentalism is and was inevitable. We went from the spoken word to the written word, to radio, to television then the computer. With each successive jump in our ability to communicate we also saw a rise of radical fundamentalist eruption.

*Discussion Question*

What can we do to resolve the problems arising from modernization and the impact it has on religious beliefs?

## Why does one become a member of a Violent Fundamentalist Cult?

There are two effects I want to tell you about concerning relationships first: The Trim Tab effect and the Boiling Frog Effect. The Trim Tab effect occurs with small changes that have large effects. The Trim Tab is at the bottom of the rudder of a large sailboat. The rudder is what moves the boat, but the trim tab is what moves the rudder. No one has the strength to move the rudder, so a trim tab is necessary. It is in the small changes to a relationship that bring people into agreement.

Have you ever wondered why a spouse would stay in an abusive relationship? Alternatively, how they got there? They normally got there because of small-unnoticed changes in the relationship. Thus the Boiling Frog: If you throw a frog into a pan of water that is boiling, it jumps out. If you put it into a pan of cold water and slowly turn up the heat, it stays until it is dead. Bad relationships are like that usually. They start with innocuous yet somewhat painful jokes, and then more painful statements that are derogatory…from name calling it goes to rough handling, from rough handling to an occasional hit, from a hit to a beating…and so on.

The induction into a cult has a similar trail it follows. Yet the inductee though at the early stages cut off from finding other sources of that which might help them break free they are then indoctrinated, usually slowly and incrementally to believing a system of violence and arrogance and to value the group they are a part of more than anything else in the world.

Fundamentalists' are threatened by modernity and the changes it brings to their culture because it challenges their belief system, which in turns challenges the way they attempt to live their lives. The introduction of the written word brought about democracies and the absolutists used violence in an effort to maintain authority for as long as they could. Threatened by a rising tide of monistic voices from their subjects that they should be able to talk to God and read God's words for themselves.

Fundamentalists are threatened by modernity from the entire major religions, primarily from Islamic, Christian and Judaist. Their response that leads to violence begins with taking the mythos of their scriptures and attempting to make it into a political strategy that makes logical sense to them. They see themselves in the middle of a great battle between good and evil itself. They being on the side of good and all who in their mind oppose them; are evil and attempting to trick them with facts. This in turn justifies their use of a militant piety that usually results in violence wherein they believe they are only defending themselves and doing the work of G-d or God or Allah. In all of these religions, the use of literal interpretation of their scriptures is a relatively new event in their religions. The interpretations of allegorical statements in their scriptures remained in the realm of clearly understood allegory until the early 16th century for the majority with few exceptions (The 16th century is the beginning of Technological Innovations that started the Industrial Revolution.) The danger comes from taking the mythos of the meaning of allegory and instead of allowing it to influence ones thinking and clear ones judgment turn it into a blueprint for developing political strategies making all who think different opponents, subjects or targets.

*Discussion Question*

What is one thing you would say to a person considering committing violence in the name of their religion?

## *Logos versus Mythos*

I did a charcoal drawing of a unicorn crying that fed the waters of the flood during the time of Noah. I drew it about 18 years ago, it is unpublished. It was titled "Job Chapter 39," Job chapter 39 mentions the unicorn. The human mind although it is dependent on the use of logic to analyze problems does not use logic in thinking, for the most part. We think heuristically or rather in stories. The human mind is capable of putting 1 + 1 together and easily seeing the answer is 2. However, because of our ability to also use mythos we can synergize. Synergy allows us to add 1 + 1 and come up with the seemingly illogical number of 3 (by thinking outside the box).

Examples: 1 apple plus 1 apple equals 2 apples; 1 mammal plus 1 mammal equals 3 mammals when they reproduce.

*Logos* or logic is to rational thinking, what Myth or *mythos* is to reflective thinking. Both are needed for a clear understanding of religion or of science; without a balanced knowledge of both abilities then we have occurrences such as "Scientific Materialism" (no possibility of supernatural explanations) or "Mysticism" (no possibility of natural explanations) occurring unregulated and with harmful effects. The best of both aspects is what most people aim for their own spiritual and mental health.

*Discussion Question*

Can we remain logical and still have a belief in the supernatural?

## *Why do you think Discrimination exists in religious settings?*

OK, here is how I look at it: People are human; and even though they develop a higher consciousness, and develop morally, we remain human. We begin life as a baby, we cry, food appears, and our diaper is changed. As a baby, we see ourselves as the center of the world. We are egocentric, and we go from a child to a young adult. We view our family then as the center of "the world" and we become ethnocentric. From that point, we become adults and we begin to view humankind, still as the "center of the world," and we are anthropomorphic.

Being anthropomorphic; when we see volcanoes erupt; we say, "The volcano is angry." The nature of humans is to see anyone and anything outside of themselves as having importance if they 1) Add value to their "own life" 2) Support their cultural view, without challenging it and 3) Hold to the level of importance they feel about themselves in the universe. Some religious viewpoints are seen as "more logical" than others. Therefore, dominant religions come about because the majorities see how these beliefs support their perception of reality. Humans will only accept something they comprehend even if it is symbolically.

When there is a prejudicial harmful discrimination in any organization, even religious ones. It is because of the lack of development of those who display the behavior. I have inserted below a copy of James Fowlers' presentation on the "Stages of Faith." His work is similar to that of Lawrence Kohlbergs level moral maturity, and Jane Loevingers' nine stages of ego development.

Why is there discrimination? Because the people who discriminate "…Know not what they do…" They lack the maturation needed for them to make clear and decisive responses that are morally courageous.


*Discussion Question*

Why do you think Discrimination exists in religious settings?

Along those line I hope this helps…

Levels of Enlightenment

How about this? First, assuming spiritual enlightenment exists and it is not merely psychological enlightenment nor moral maturity we are talking about: There can be a number of degrees recognized or applied to spiritual enlightenment to see where someone is along the spectrum of enlightenment.

Second, assuming that spiritual enlightenment exists then it is available to everyone that has a spirit regardless of age, race, gender and so forth. The third assumption is that spiritual enlightenment is linked to "faith." This is not merely monotheistic faith, but faith in general. If that is the case then the work of James Fowler can have utility to answer of how one knows someone is spiritually enlightened.

Stage One: Intuitive/Projective; this stage is marked by the rise of imagination. It is a stage of rapid growth and long lasting effects.

Stage Two: Mythic/Literal; Here are the beginnings of the ability to evaluate and narrate fantasy and imagination. They often take symbols, stories and myths at their face value yet are moved at a deep level by the meaning and purpose.

Stage Three: Synthetic/Conventional; this is marked by the beginning of what Jeanne Piaget called "operational thinking." It means we can think about our own thinking. It is at this stage that we can see an image of God as an extension of an interpersonal relationship. (I need to add here that a Buddhist or Taoist might see this as the stage that one can sense their connection to the supernatural. *The word "Taoist" is pronounced "Daoist" and often written as such.*)

Stage Four: Individuative/Projective; for those who achieve it this is a stage where one sees they have been "pushed out from" or individuated from their interpersonal relationships. The saying from Santayana is offered here to help; "We do not know who discovered water first, but we know it was not fish." Here is the stage where boundaries are looked at or "where you end and I begin." It is the beginning of conviction and a sense of authenticity.

Stage Five: Conjunctive Faith; at stage four, one examines boundaries; at stage five one begins to examine the permeability between boundaries and reflectively examine the myths and taboos of the collective unconscious. Intimacy becomes more important and relationships become broader more in-depth crossing socio-cultural boundaries with ease. It is a period where paradox becomes understandable and it is recognized that truth has multiple aspects.

Stage Six: Universalizing Faith; this is where one experiences a shift from the self as the center of experience or of reality. They appear more lucid and simple than they are in reality. They also appear liberating, *to those who exist below stage four they do not exist or they appear in a magical sense.* Fowler said they have the quality of "relevant irrelevance." "Their *subversiveness* makes our compromises show up as they are."

Reference: http://www.lifespirals.com/TheMindSpiral/Fowler/fowler.html

## *Did Buddha have Faith?*

We will go over many aspects of the way other people have answered some "tough questions" as we progress through class. Each of us though, is ultimately responsible for our own answers on these thought provoking questions.

Can we prove the existence of God, gods or an intelligent force, even a supernatural force?

Why do bad things happen to good people?

The first deals with the level of understanding in logic, the second deals with the logic of our level of understanding. If we come to a point that we actually can prove the existence of God, (I have many people's ideas of such proofs); what then becomes of faith?

All of the monotheistic religions and most of the others appear hinged on the utility of faith. For the theists it seems to many that if ones faith is *unshakable*, that God exists; they can ask the proverb-producing question then, "From whence cometh evil?" In the Christian Bible in the book of Job, Job had a long conversation with God. Job was actually the last recorded human alive to talk with God in the lineage of the King James and the Duouay Rheims versions.

God explained to Job, when Job was asking God why He had allowed his entire family and all that he owned to be taken away; that Job's (your) thoughts are not my thoughts...He asked Job some actual "science" questions, one of which was about the formation of wind...Job had no answer. The writing signifies that sometimes we see things as "bad" when God does not, because God sees the bigger picture, which we as of yet have hidden from us.

In Buddhism, there is writing, of the Buddha telling a woman who has lost a child. The woman asked the Buddha to bring the child back to life. The Buddha said he could do it but that he needed a cup of salt from a household that no one had been lost to death in. Therefore, she went house to house and asked everyone. She returned and told the Buddha that there was no such household.

The Buddha then explained the process of death was a part of life not the other way around, life is not ended by death but it is its culmination point for this reality. Personally, I believe that though it is impossible to prove the existence of God. God is the Author all truth. I believe that it does not matter where one hears truth even if it came from a rock. If it is truth then it is truth; there is a statement of logic in law for evidence. It is *Res Ipsa Loquitor*, it means the thing speaks for itself, the validity of "real truth" is self-evident...e.g. as the Christian apostle Paul spoke of faith "being the substance of things hoped, the evidence of things not seen..." "Theory" is to Science what "Mythos" is to Religion. There are certain things that can be proven in science and certain things that can only be hypothesized. Similarly, there are certain things in religion that are fact and certain things that can only be "believed."

*Discussion Question*

Did Buddha have faith or was it a true enlightened or supreme knowledge? Can what the Buddha teaches be "proven" in a court of law or in a laboratory scientifically?

### *Religious Pluralism and Interfaith Dialogue "Some Thoughts"* Thoughts"

Most of us in our "hurry up and wait" lives search for an easy answer to life's problems. We usually want a checklist that we can follow that will guarantee our success in any endeavor whether it is in our relationships with others or in our seeking of transcendence. We want something that works all of the time and under every circumstance. We want something concrete and factual yet it allows for growth and change even transcendence and revelation for others and ourselves.

In life, there is no cookie cutter answer to life's problems other than life itself. The mystery of "Life" explains itself many ways and all of them can be right. We can have a "one way" mentality and still be open-minded without being empty headed. For open mindedness to occur we must know ourselves first, we must know "what, how and why" we see things as we see them.

The Study of Interfaith Dialogue

I have to say this of myself and for others that we can look at religion as students and simply codify, classify and relegate the ideas into simple understandable terms to remember and recite, however it does no one any good except to pass a test in a class. People need to have a sense of confidence in their beliefs and in their own self that they can actually have a dialogue with others who have beliefs that truly differ from their own without fearing a loss of their self-identity.

It is obvious that even in this setting of online instruction that many people have taken the concepts, they have newly learned from other religions, Buddhism and Christianity for one example and have come up with new ideas for a new mythos and it has even affected their logos or their view on how to behave or act. The people of Israel posed the question of "How they will then live?" to the prophet Ezekiel when told to change their ways. We naturally ask that question whenever we see alternatives that extend beyond our own narrow scope of life.

I cannot allow my faith to affect my behavior in such a way that I discriminate against others unfairly to make it so that my words, my demeanor, or my actions are such that they portray disrespect for those that believe differently from me. I know that I am of a certain conviction and I know that because of that knowledge of my condition I can keep myself from a discriminatory attitude and behavior that will make me an obnoxious pest at best and a fundamentalist dictator at worst. I want neither for my life nor for the lives of those whom I am connected to in any manner.

Thus, I must speak out against such things and point out that there is a way to have your spiritual beliefs whatever they may be or may become and remain humane and show loving kindness to all people everywhere. I have found that people who act in a surreptitious or manipulative way in a society are often expressing a basic human dilemma that stands unmet unfulfilled or not recognized. It is my intent to make my agenda clear, compassionate and worthy of full use. Keeping this in mind, that if the world existed in perfect clarity there would be no need for stories, art, mythos, or religions. In each cosmology or cosmogony the one least deceptive is the one that is actually lived. No laws can be made against truth, love, joy or any such good thing.

When we look at the belief systems, it becomes clear it is their apparent shared paradoxes and contradictions that bring about their classification; each has a symbiosis. The Totalitarian Absolutist does not use totalitarianism to base their values on; they base them on the misperceptions of the Liberal; the Charismatic Mystic's values on that of the untenable dogma of the Orthodox; the Militant Fundamentalist on the inflexible orthopraxy of the Absolutist. Integrity needs no rules or values. It is a principle and principles unlike our religious politics, stand-alone being self-sufficient.

Overly justified by the monistic as inherent and equally disqualified by the monotheist as ineffable. When the meaning of life seems hidden, even suppressed, you know it is still there. You are the proof it is still there, for you are alive and that in itself carries the "holy grail," the hope, the essence of the search.

It is the lock opening as the Key turns.

We each have a right to believe that the truth when written with a capital letter is still of a relative nature as opposed to an absolute. Nevertheless, as Winston Churchill pointed out that degradation of truth does not change the facts. Whosoever purposefully uses words to confuse others to gain an unfair advantage is showing their intent to allow tyranny to exist. The study of religion is the study of the hearts of others, where you come to know them intimately.

Humans can disagree without being disagreeable and we can agree without losing who we are or being untrue to ourselves. It is my hope for each of you that your dialogue with others who see differently from you is that it enriches your life and theirs.

Sometimes the message of the story is the most important aspect. The majority of what we read to our children has some message in it for them. It is also the "way" we read it to them that helps transfer our beliefs and values. I can understand the Fundamentalist position about the literal truth of the Word of God concerning the Christian bible. Often the statement has been made when posing the possibility that certain aspects may be story, parable or allegory to get across a point that one is "questioning the Word of Gawd." (The use of the term Gawd in this is often as if God is being summoned.) It is not that the Word of God is being questioned actually but the position that the Fundamentalists are taking and the interpretation of the scripture they are reading. When arguing over whether a story is myth of fact one can waste time looking for the speck of dust in another's eye while overlooking the log of wood in one's own, as well as truly miss the impact of the story itself.

There are certain parts of every sacred scripture that are based on natural laws as well as spiritual principles. Nearly every religion has instructions for the understanding of their scriptures as well as the application. When one seeks to take the mythos of a scripture and apply it politically problems normally arise. It is similar to taking the infinite and attempting to fit it into the finite. The mythos deals with that which is abstract or hard to understand. It is often relayed in stories sometimes they are true and sometimes they are not. The purpose of the story is to convey a truth that is usually global in scope. It is not relevant that the story is actually true when the purpose of telling the story is to convey a meaning, or natural law or a principle. There is usually; logos in all sacred scriptures as well. To understand the logos the statement has to be true in and of it-self. For instance the idea that Jesus Christ or Buddha or Mohammed existed is presented as logos in their scriptures. Some of the stories told are told to convey a meaning more important than the story itself, this is mythos. Christian have several passages telling them how to interpret the scriptures. Paul told Timothy "Study to show thyself approved unto God, a workman that needeth not be ashamed, rightly dividing the word of truth." (2 Timothy 2:15) I think they need to have an understanding of relative truth versus absolute truth as well as the socio-cultural influences involved then and now.

They need to know who the particular scripture passages were written to, and then the context of what was actually written before they extrapolate global axioms. If they do the process the other way they can make it mean anything they want to a much larger degree. They could end up confusing the meaning of what was said with what was meant as happened many times in the scriptures themselves: Christ's Bodily Temple confused with the earthly temple, John 2:20; The New Birth confused with the physical birth John, 3:4; The Water of Life confused with physical water, John 4:15; Spiritual Nourishment confused with food, John 4:33; Absorbing Christ's Spirit with eating His literal body and drinking His literal blood, John 6:52. These are examples used in the scriptures to explain what I am speaking of. They show how confusion in logic leads to misinterpretation.

It is hard to sometimes walk away from a problem in order to solve it. Sometimes our burdens seem so great that they are irresolvable. I have learned this from the study of Logic: To actually know that a problem exists there needs to be some form of a solution to base it on that it exists. As in Physics we cannot measure darkness, so we used Mythos to describe the darkness, even the darkness of our minds. Mythos predates and is the ancestor of our modern Psychologies. The problems we find hardest to walk away from are those that cause us to feel dread. What is easiest to change is the feeling of dread. There was a reference to this, in one of the books called "Chicken Soup for the Soul." A story was told about a woman who had wrecked the car and she dreaded telling her husband. She finally told him and she was shocked he was not upset. He explained, he could be upset or not upset and it would not change what happened to the car. In addition, if he did get upset it would only hide his fear that he could have lost his wife in a car wreck. He explained that instead of being upset I have chosen to be happy that you are alive. We can buy a new car. This story is not a one size fits all but this saying fits most problems: If there are no solutions, then there are no problems... Violent punishment is a deterrent only for certain types of cultures.

A culture that promotes education is less influenced by strong punishments to deter them from crime. They are more influenced by the positive aspects of the rewards for normative behavior. As the society progresses and produces autonomy they are more influenced by the egalitarian behavior of their people than by their laws. When any people attempt to take the mythos of evil and good fighting and polemically place it into a political agenda they will fail. The problem arises because the infinite cannot be leveraged by the finite in that way. Mythos serves to guide and influence the behavior of a people, it is not meant to become a political strategy. Logos is what is used for political strategies that work. We as humans tend to "demonize" people we do not understand or when something they do is criminally wrong. Even those who are secular do this very thing. The demonizing attributes that we are in the struggle of good and evil. This exaggeration exacerbates the problem and starts a triangle of abusiveness (eye for an eye type attitude) and then a rescuer mode (where "good" people step in for a while; "heroes") and then back to being victims (feeling helpless because good did not triumph and the world is not in Shangri-La). All it takes is to break one part of the cycle and people "wake up" so to speak.

A few others that have tried to blend the natural lustful part of humanity with religious experience are the Celtics through the worship of Achtland, the Africans through the worship of Luamerava, the Chinese through P'an Chin-lien (a goddess of Brothels, Prostitution), the Phillipines through Tagabayan (adultery, incest), and the Mayans through Xtabay (seduction). In the west the Puritan influence caused a backlash against too strict of a moral influence turning it into a seeming facade of purity. The cloistered nuns of many Catholic and some Buddhist religions are required to have "experienced the world" before they take their vows. Carl Gustav Jung believed we have a dark side and thus developed therapies to deal with the shadow side of human nature. His proposition was that to keep the "monster caged" it needed to be fed some crumbs (recognition only) so that it was too weak to escape but not dies. For the loss of the natural part of one's' humanity was the loss of self. Jung was a contemporary of Freud and he also did a great deal of research into dreams and dreaming. His concepts of "archetypes" emerging from dreams stemmed from his research into the Tinglit Eskimos, the rainforest Indians, and the Australian aborigines. Jung held that archetypes bridged time and space in the absence of a known method of communication. Joseph Campbell author of "The Hero with a Thousand Faces" and the "Power of Myth" took Jung's concepts a step further and traced the archetypes of all the major known religions of the world. Campbell's concepts' of the "hero's journey" (seeking truth) was one of the sources for the trilogy of "Star Wars" by George Lucas.

"People say that what we're all seeking is a meaning for life. I don't think that's what we're really seeking. I think that what we're seeking is an experience of being alive, so that our life experiences on the purely physical plane will have resonances within our own innermost being and reality, so that we actually feel the rapture of being alive." --Joseph Campbell, The Power of Myth (1988)

There was a belief held by the Catholic Church that left-handedness was of the devil. About ten percent of the American population is left-handed. In Japan it was grounds for divorce up until about two decades ago to be left-handed.

For the Christian denominations who held to this fallacy it was often based on Matthew 6:3 where it talks about "not letting your left know what your right hand is doing." You can read more about this at the following web site:

http://www.geocities.com/Athens/Acropolis/1684/lefthand.html

As we learn more about the "facts" of reality faith becomes more defined. Faith is different from mere belief in that faith is built on compassion, moral integrity and moral courage. Beliefs can be built on desires, wants and even needs...Compassionate belief systems appear to be built on the search for truth: Whereas, uncompassionate belief systems appear to be challenged by the presentation of truth and of change.

There is a famous question in the study of Religious Ethics: "When is it right to do wrong?" Dr Martin Luther King is a living testimony of a good answer to this question.

*Discussion Question*

In your opinion; "When is it right to do wrong? or Is it ever right to do wrong?" (Consider the answer from the Fundamentalist viewpoint, and then from the Conservative religious establishment viewpoint.)

## Science: "Is Science always Logical?" "How our Mythos has influenced Science?"

"In the US, according to a survey published in Nature in 1997, four out of 10 scientists believe in God. Just over 45% said they did not believe, and 14.5% described themselves as doubters or agnostics. This ratio of believers to non believers had not changed in 80 years." this is an excerpt from an article on the following web site:

http://www.guardian.co.uk/life/feature/story/0,13026,1034872,00.html

There is a difference between the mythos of scriptures and the logos of science and of fact. There is both logos and mythos in both Science and in Scriptures; however, there is normally even today more mythos in scriptures. Logos cannot soothe a broken heart or calm fears that are existential or answer questions there are as of yet there are no answers for. Sir Francis Bacon counselor to King James wrote in his "Advancement of Learning," in 1605 that "All truth, even the most sacred doctrines of religion, must be subjected to the stringent critical methods of empirical science. If they contradicted proven facts and evidence of our senses, they must be cast aside." Sir Francis Bacon did not speak of science as we do today. When we talk of science, we include the idea of Hypothesis and of guessing to figure things out. He only looked at science as that of collecting facts and what our five senses could be aware of. The western cultures view of religion was further altered shortly thereafter by Rene Descartes, and then Thomas Hobbes diminishing the view of mythos as having utility until John Locke as well as Blaise Pascal held proposed that science supported religion. The authors of the constitution of the United States particularly those who wrote it were strongly influenced by the writing of these men Pascal and Locke. Blaise Pascal is famous for Pascals Wager, where he postulates that it is safer to believe in God than not believe in

God because to not believe in God it is stated will bring harm even damnation, but to believe in God can do no harm. Though it is not a truly sound logic it has very strong merit. It carries both the mythos and the logos of belief to a stage of where we are today ontologically. (Ontology is the study of the proof of God and of existence itself.)

### Social Aspects of Lyths: "What effect has Mythos had on our behavior?"

We can each have our own unique perspective on the truth. The thing is having a unique perspective like having an accent; each of us can say the very same thing in a very different way. This is relative truth; now absolute truth exists as represented by the fact that although we each are saying the same thing in a different way: we are each saying the same thing.

"Imagine all of us looking at the sky...we are all looking at a star...since one of you is in Florida, one in Virginia and so on, we all see the same star from a different perspective. It will have a different hue because of the atmospheres we see it through...however, we all see a star...if one person says they see a cow...will that will cause it to become a cow?" The truth when known brings about a certainty of knowledge that does not lead to self-righteousness and angry mannerisms.

It leads to a love that allows for a positive tension. A loving person allows others to disagree with what they believe; sometimes they even turn the other cheek. People that know truth act in a morally responsible manner. They are able to explain to those who see stars and not cows what they believe and it makes sense to those that hear them. They are able to separate mythos and logos in such a way to detract from neither.

This allows the crowd to remain independent, and decentralized. Both of these are important for a group of people to have a functional collective intelligence. It allows them to communicate to each other, to talk about those things that will allow them to realize the truth.

## Are all Cultures driven by a Mythos?

OK, here is how I look at it: People are human; and even though they develop a higher consciousness, and develop morally, we remain human. We begin life as a baby, we cry, food appears, and our diaper is changed. As a baby, we see ourselves as the center of the world. We are egocentric, and we go from a child to a young adult. We view our family then as the center of "the world" and we become ethnocentric. From that point, we become adults and we begin to view humankind, still as the "center of the world," and we are anthropomorphic.

Being anthropomorphic; when we see volcanoes erupt; we say, "The volcano is angry." The nature of humans is to see anyone and anything outside of themselves as having importance if they 1) Add value to their "own life" 2) Support their cultural view, without challenging it and 3) Hold to the level of importance they feel about themselves in the universe. Some religious viewpoints are seen as "more logical" than others. Therefore, dominant religions come about because the majorities see how these beliefs support their perception of reality.

Humans will only accept something they comprehend even if it is symbolically.

People often turn to religion in times of trouble, stress or crisis if their cultural view of religion is that it is an outside source of strength. When a community or a society does not allow by social norms, customs or even law any part of their social health inducing aspects, or races, genders and so forth full functionality to their highest capability this common problem ensues.

Religion is an inner source of strength that is not merely "turned to" in times of trouble for a strong society. The strength is derived from the openness and the acceptance of change and of questioning and of finding suitable answers. Autonomy is sought for all people in healthy societies and the religion will reflect that in its precepts and teachings in both its mythos and its logos.

As countries modernize, they experience change with varying degrees of conflict involved. Countries that have modernization occur rapidly are hotbeds for Fundamentalist movements. They are especially vulnerable if they are Third World Nations, who lack a system of national education. There appears to be a strong correlation to technological/educational growth to religious abatement (MacCulloch, Pezzini).

As Europe and America moved into the Industrial age, they did their changes gradually. Each technological improvement brought about a correspondent change in their overall social make-up. The reliance on mythos faded or sublimated to the use of reason. Luther saw the emergence of reason as a detriment to the growth of Christianity that it would lead to Atheism. Calvin saw it as an empirically supporting the Christian doctrinal beliefs and so did John Wesley who brought about the "Methodical Christian Approach" and the Methodist church. (Armstrong) Karen Armstrong proposed that the very reasoning they use to understand the significance of religion and faith has blinded secularists and those who follow the scientific rationalistic approach to life (Scientific Materialism). The secularist approach has led to an arrogance that kept them in a position of trying to "be right" when "doing right" was needed for understanding. That these theologies and ideologies may be rooted in fear is apparent, but modern secularism is the culprit, having drained life of its meaning and purpose. With the encroachment of secular ideologies, a form of paranoia erupts in highly religious peoples. When the interpretations of meaning behind discoveries are prone to dismantle long held unquestioned suppositions about reality, fear is inevitable. As Armstrong points out "millions of people around the globe struggle with seemingly irreconcilable philosophies of life, the rise of militant fundamentalism is and was inevitable." We went from the spoken word to the written word, to radio, to television then the computer. With each successive jump in our ability to communicate we also saw a rise of radical fundamentalist eruption.

*Discussion Question*

What can we do to resolve the problems arising from modernization and the impact it has on religious beliefs?

## Bibliography

Boston: Houghton Mifflin Co., 1986. ISBN 0-395-53008-3 (pp. 235-236).

Crown: New York., 1984. ISBN 0-517-55407-0 (pp. 148-149).

New York: Lippincott & Crowell, 1980. ISBN 0-690-01685-9 (p. 140).

*Reuters.* 6 March 1992.

*The Boston Globe.* 7 March 1994 (p. 30).

*The New York Times.* 13 March 1988 (p. B31).

*The New York Times.* 24 March 1986 (p. C18).

*The Vancouver Sun.* 21 February 1992 (Diary; p. D2).

(1993). *Sex: the myth and the magic*. Boise, Idaho: Pacific Press Pub. Association.

(1997). Retrieved January 30, 2007, from Western Oregon University Web site: http://www.wou.edu/las/physci/ch412/perhist.htm

(2003) Semiotics. (n.d.) The American Heritage® Dictionary of the English Language, Fourth Edition. (2003). Retrieved January 30 2007 from http://www.thefreedictionary.com/semiotics

Alice Low ; illustrated by Arvis Stewart. (1994). *The Macmillan book of Greek gods and heroes*. New York: Maxwell Macmillan International.

Association, M., & University of South Africa. (1993). *Myth and interdisciplinary studies*. Pretoria: University of South Africa.

Atlan, H. (1993). *Enlightenment to enlightenment: intercritique of science and myth.*

Albany: State University of New York Press.

Ausband, Stephen C. (1983). *Myth and meaning, myth and order*. Macon, Ga.: Mercer University Press.

Australian aboriginal mythology: essays in honour of W. E. H. Stanner (economic fallacies) *Australian aboriginal mythology: essays in honour of W. E. H. Stanner*.

Bannister, Robert C. (1979). *Social Darwinism: science and myth in Anglo-American social thought*. Philadelphia: Temple University Press.

Barksdale, E. C. (1980). *Cosmologies of consciousness: science and literary myth in an exploration of the beginnings and development of mind*. Cambridge, Mass.: Schenkman Pub. Co.

Barnet, S., & Bedau, H. (1996). *Current issues and enduring questions: a guide to critical thinking and argument, with readings* (4th ed.). Boston: Bedford Books of St. Martin's Press.

Blary, L., & al, e. (1976). *Myth and ideology in American culture*: *Publications de l'Universitâe de Lille*. Lille: Amâericaines et Canadiennes, Universitâe de Lille.

Bloomfield, Morton W. (1981). *Allegory, myth, and symbol*. Cambridge, Mass.: Harvard University Press.

Blumenberg, H. (1985). *Work on myth*. Cambridge, Mass.: MIT Press.

Bondi, H. (1967). *Assumption and myth in physical theory*. London: Cambridge U.P.

Bonosky, P. (1967). *Beyond the borders of myth, from Vilnius to Hanoi*. New York: Praxis Press.

Booss, C. (1986). *A Treasury of Irish myth, legend, and folklore*. New York: Crown Publishers.

(Polar bears like it hot: a guide to popular misconceptions)
*Polar bears like it hot: a guide to popular misconceptions*.

Abell, Derek F. (1980). *Defining the business: the starting point of strategic planning*. Englewood Cliffs, N.J.: Hall.

Agg, W. (1997). *A litany of popular misconceptions*. Hawthorn: Hudson.

Alper, w. (1998). *The "God" part of the brain: a scientific interpretation of human spirituality and God*. Boulder, Colo.?: Rogue Press.

Arens, W., & Montague, S. P. (1981). *The American dimension: cultural myths and social realities* (2nd ed.). Sherman Oaks, CA: Alfred Pub. Co.

Armstrong, K. (2000, August). *www.ChristianEthicsToday.com*. Retrieved March 7, 2007, from The Christian Ethics Today Foundation Web site: http://www.christianethicstoday.com/Issue/029/TheBattleForGodByKarenArmstrong_029_29_.htm This was a Book Review by Darold Morgan, Richardson, Texas. In it he states, "Many secularists and devotees of a scientific approach to life have been unable to grasp the importance of religion to the faithful." The review as well as Armstrongs book are well worth reading.

Armstrong, K. (2005). *A short history of myth*. New York: Canongate.

Armstrong, Karen (2001), "The Battle for God," Random House Publishing

Barbara and David P. Mikkelson. (1996, February 27). White Wilderness. Retrieved March 7, 2007, from Urban

Legends Reference Pages Web site:
http://www.snopes.com/disney/films/lemmings.htm

Barbara and David P. Mikkelson. (1996, February 27). *White Wilderness*. Retrieved March 7, 2007, from Urban Legends Reference Pages Web site:
http://www.snopes.com/disney/films/lemmings.htm

Berne, E. (1976). *Beyond games and scripts*. New York: Random House.

Bloom, H. (1995). *The Lucifer principle: a scientific expedition into the forces of history*. New York: Atlantic Monthly Press.

Bloom, H. (2000). *The global brain: the evolution of mass mind from the big bang to the 21st century*. New York: Wiley.

Bottici, C. (2007). *A philosophy of political myth*. New York: Cambridge University Press.

Bowers, C.A. (1993). *Education, cultural myths, and the ecological crisis: toward deep changes*: *SUNY series in the philosophy of education*. Albany, N.Y.: State University of New York Press.

Bowie, A.M. (1993). *Aristophanes: myth, ritual, and comedy*. New York, NY: Cambridge University Press.

Boym, S. (1991). *Death in quotation marks: cultural myths of the modern poet*. Cambridge, Mass: Harvard University Press.

Brockway, Robert W. (1993). *Myth from the Ice Age to Mickey Mouse*. Albany: State University of New York Press.

Brooke Noel Moore. (1991 [i.e. c1992). *Critical thinking* (3rd ed.). Mountain View, Calif.: Mayfield Pub. Co.

Brown, O. G. (1994). *Debunking the myth: stories of African-American university students*. Bloomington, Ind.: Phi Delta Kappa Educational Foundation.

Browne, M. N., & Keeley, S. M. (1986). *Asking the right questions: a guide to critical thinking* (2nd ed.). Englewood Cliffs, N.J.: Hall.

Broyles, J. (2006). *Egyptian mythology*. New York: Rosen Pub. Group.

Bryant, J. (1979). *A new system: or, An analysis of ancient mythology*. New York: Garland Pub.

Buchler, I. R., & Selby, H. A. (1968). *A formal study of myth*: *University of Texas. Center for Intercultural Studies in Folklore and Oral History. Monograph series*. Austin: University of Texas.

Burnam, Tom. More Misinformation. By Nwankwo Ezeabasili. (1977). *African science: myth or reality*. New York: Vantage Press.

By R. Larry Moyer. (2004). *21 things God never said: correcting our misconceptions about evangelism*. Grand Rapids, MI: Kregel Publications.

Cairns, D. (1960). *A gospel without myth? Bultmann's challenge to the preacher*: *The Preacher's library*. London: SCM Press.

Castellon, F. (1948). *Mythology: The age of fable; or, Stories of gods and heroes*. Garden City, N.Y.: Doubleday.

Chang, K.C. (1983). *Art, myth, and ritual: the path to political authority in ancient China*. Cambridge, Mass.: Harvard University Press.

Charle, Suzanne. "Television; Hunting Wildlife with a Movie Camera."

Chester, M. (1978). *Particles: an introduction to particle physics*. New York: Macmillan.

Cogan, R. (1998). *Critical thinking: step by step*. Lanham, Md.: University Press of America.

Coghlan, R. (1979). *Dictionary of Irish myth and legend*. Bangor: Donard Pub. Co.

Cole, P. (2006). *The myth of evil: demonizing the enemy*. Westport, Conn.: Praeger.

Combs, A., & Holland, M. (1990). *Synchronicity: science, myth, and the trickster*: *An Omega book*. New York: Paragon House.

Conner, R. P., David Hatfield Sparks, & Sparks, M. (1997). *Cassell's encyclopedia of queer myth, symbol, and spirit: gay, lesbian, bisexual, and transgender lore*. Herndon, VA: Cassell.

Cook, A. (1980). *Myth and language*. Bloomington: Indiana University Press.

Corry, John. "'Cruel Camera', About Animal Abuse." cover, R. L. A. ;., & interior art by Phil Foglio. (1987). *Myth-nomers and im-pervections*. Norfolk, Va.: Donning.

Cowan, James C. (1970). *D. H. Lawrence's American journey; a study in literature and myth*. Cleveland: Press of Case Western Reserve University.

Cunningham, A. (1973). *The Theory of myth; six studies*. London: Sheed & Ward.

Darlington, W. (1832). *A catechism of mythology; containing a compendious history of the heathen gods and heroes, indispensable to a correct knowledge of the ancient poets and the classics: with 75 engravings. To which is added, The mythology of northern Europe, translated from the French*. Baltimore: W.R. Lucas.

Davis, Kenneth C. (2005). *Don't know much about mythology: everything you need to know about the greatest stories in human history but never learned*. New York: HarperCollins Publishers.

Davison, P., Meyersohn, R., & Shils, E. (1978). *Content and taste: religion and myth*. Teaneck, N.J.: Somerset House.

Dawkins, R. (1982). *The selfish gene*. San Francisco: Freeman.

Desmonde, William H. (1997). *Magic, myth, and money: the origin of money in religious ritual*. New York: Allworth Press.

Deutsch, H. (1969). *A psychoanalytic study of the myth of Dionysus and Apollo: two variants of the son-mother relationship*. New York: International Universities Press.

Director, K. H. (1989). *A sense of wonder--from myth to science fiction*: *Elements of literature video series*. United States.

Dixon-Kennedy, M. (1997). *European myth & legend: an A-Z of people and places*. New York: Sterling Pub.

Dixon-Kennedy, M. (1998). *Encyclopedia of Russian & Slavic myth and legend*. Santa Barbara, Calif.: CLIO.

Dobson, Geoffrey P. (2005). *A chaos of delight: science, religion and myth and the shaping of Western thought*. Oakville: Equinox Pub.

Donald Wayne Viney. (1998). *A brief guide to logic and critical thinking for nonvulcans*. Dubuque, Iowa: Kendall/Hunt Pub.

Duggan, William J. (1971). *Myth and Christian belief*. Notre Dame, Ind.: Fides.

Dunne, John S. (1973). *Time and myth*. Notre Dame: University of Notre Dame Press.

edited. (1975). Australian aboriginal mythology: essays in honour of W. E. H. Stanner. Canberra: Australian Institute of Aboriginal Studies.

edited. (1996). *Anthropology, folklore, and myth*. New York: Garland Pub.

edited. (1996). *Psychology and myth*. New York: Garland Pub.

Enwall, J. (1994?-1995). *A myth become reality: history and development of the Miao written language*. Stockholm?: Institute of Oriental Languages.

Epstein, Richard L. (1999). *Critical thinking*. Belmont, CA: Wadsworth Pub. Co.

Ezeabasili, N. (1977). *African science: myth or reality*. New York: Vantage Press.

Ferry, Jon. "Lemmings Commit Mass Murder, Not Mass Suicide."

Fisher, J. A., Black, S. J., & Daugherty, M. H. (1956). *Critical thinking and the humanities*. Boston: Boston University Press.

Foreman, Judy. "How & Why." Fowler, J. (n.d.). *My Interview with James W. Fowler on the Stages of Faith*. Retrieved March 7, 2007, from Harold Kent Straughn Web site: http://www.lifespirals.com/TheMindSpiral/Fowler/fowler.html

Fowler, J. (n.d.). *My Interview with James W. Fowler on the Stages of Faith*. Retrieved March 7, 2007, from Harold Kent Straughn Web site: http://www.lifespirals.com/TheMindSpiral/Fowler/fowler.html

Fowler, J. (n.d.). *My Interview with James W. Fowler on the Stages of Faith*. Retrieved March 7, 2007, from Harold Kent Straughn Web site: http://www.lifespirals.com/TheMindSpiral/Fowler/fowler.html

Janis, Irving L. (1982). *Groupthink: psychological studies of policy decisions and fiascoes* (2nd ed. , rev.). Boston: Houghton Mifflin.

Judge, A. (1980, June). *Utilisation of International Documentation*. Retrieved March 7, 2007, from Creative Commons Attribution-NonCommercial-NoDerivs 2.5 License. Web site: http://www.laetusinpraesens.org/docs80s/80utilen.php

(Introductory report (Panel III) for the Second World Symposium on International Documentation (Brussels, 20-22 June 1980) organized by the United Nations Institute for Training and Research (UNITAR) and the Association of International Libraries (AIL). [UNITAR/AIL/SYM.2/WP.III/Rep]. Published in *International Documents for the 80's: their role and use* (Unifo Publishers, 1982, in an incomplete version, edited by Th. Dimitrov). An abridged version also appeared as: Societal Learning and the Erosion of Collective Memory: the role of international organizations in combatting global amnesia. In: *Transnational Associations*, 36, 2, pp 83-93, bibl. Version française )

Jung, C. G. (1976). *Abstracts of The collected works of C. G. Jung: a guide to The collected works, volumes I-XVII, Bollinger series XX, Princeton University Press*. Rockville, Md.: Information Planning Associates.

MacCulloch, Robert and Pezzini, Silvia, (2002), "The Role of Freedom, Growth and Religion in the Taste for Revolution," http://repec.org/res2003/Pezzini.pdf [web pdf]

Maltin, Leonard. *The Disney Films.* Olsen, S. (Ed.). (1998). Retrieved January 30, 2007, from The American Donkey and Mule Society Web site: http://www.imh.org/imh/bw/donkey.html

Orriss, M. (2004). *Karpman Drama Triangle*. Retrieved March 7, 2007, from Coaching Supervision Academy Web site: http://www.coachingsupervisionacademy.com/our_approach/karpman_drama_triangle.phtml

Poundstone, William. *Bigger Secrets.*

Sagi, Douglas. "Scientists Demolish Lemming Legends."

Silva, P. C., & Moe, R. L. (2000-2004). Retrieved January 30, 2007, from McGraw-Hill Encyclopedia of Science & Technology Online Web site: http://http://www.accessscience.com/Encyclopedia/7/73/Est_736800_frameset.html?doi

Surowiecki, J. (2004). *The wisdom of crowds: why the many are smarter than the few and how collective wisdom shapes business, economies, societies, and nations*. New York: Doubleday :.

This was a Book Review by Darold Morgan, Richardson,Texas. In it he states "Many secularists and devotees of a scientific approach to life have been unable to grasp the importance of religion to the faithful." The review as well as Armstrongs book are well worth reading.

Toffler, A. (1985). *The third wave*. New York: Hill.

## About the Author

Frank Mueller

Frank Mueller was a military liaison and consultant for over ten years between the US Army and FEMA at the county level. He served twenty-one plus years of service with the USARNG, USAR, US Army serving as a Medical officer, Logistics officer, Infantry officer and Chemical officer. The majority of the time with the US Army NG was as a Chemical Officer at the Brigade and Division level advising General Staff officers on matters of Nuclear, Biological and Chemical defense. He has completed CAS3, Infantry Basic and Chemical Advanced Courses US Army, and Command and General Staff College. He worked several years in the private sector in security and protection, contracting with several US government agencies.

He has also served as an advisor for over ten years to college students seeking to satisfy their bachelor degree. He has a Master's of Science in Management from Oakland City University. He has been teaching college since 1996. He has taught in the Online Environment, the traditional college campus as well as for the Department of Correction, US Army, FEMA and written curriculum for the Indiana State Police.

He has taught as well as written curriculum in the areas of Group and Organizational Behavior, Technology, World Religions, Online Learning, Strategic Thinking, Ethics, Management, Business Communication, Economics and Financial Systems, Human Resource Management, Effective Interpersonal Relationships, Principles of Security, Systems Management, Logistics and Strategic Planning, Seminar "Successful Entrepreneur's", Managerial Quality Assurance, Macroeconomics in a Global Environment, Values: Personal and Social, Management History and Current Practice, Technology Communication and Decision Making, Management of Information Systems. He has been a member of Society for Human Resource Management (SHRM) American Society for Industrial Security (ASIS). He assisted in development Legislation to offer all National Guard of Indiana full college tuition reimbursement. (Accepted and implemented by the Military Department of Indiana and the State legislature.)

www.ingramcontent.com/pod-product-compliance
Lightning Source LLC
Chambersburg PA
CBHW041515220426
43668CB00002B/28